Rookie
Read-About® Science

Raccoons

By Allan Fowler

Consultants

Linda Cornwell, Coordinator of School Quality
and Professional Improvement
Indiana State Teachers Association

Jan Jenner, Ph.D.

◀P▶ Children's Press®
A Division of Grolier Publishing
New York London Hong Kong Sydney
Danbury, Connecticut

Visit Children's Press® on the Internet at:
http://publishing.grolier.com

Designer: Herman Adler Design Group
Photo Researcher: Caroline Anderson
The photo on the cover of this books shows a young raccoon in the woods.

Library of Congress Cataloging-in-Publication Data

Fowler, Allan.
    Raccoons / by Allan Fowler.
      p. cm. — (Rookie read-about science)
    Includes index.
    Summary: Describes the physical characteristics, habitat, life
cycle, and behavior of raccoons.
    ISBN 0-516-21590-6 (lib. bdg.)   0-516-27056-7 (pbk.)
    1. Raccoons—Juvenile literature. [1. Raccoons.] I. Titles.
II. Series.
QL737.C26F68   2000   98-52944
599.76'32—dc21   CIP
                                        AC

GROLIER
PUBLISHING

Have you ever worn a mask on Halloween?

A raccoon has black fur around its eyes.

It looks like it is wearing a mask.

A raccoon's fur is gray
or brownish gray.

It has a bushy tail with
black rings.

Raccoons are about
24 to 36 inches long,
including the tail.

Raccoons have five
toes with sharp claws
on each paw.

A raccoon uses its
front paws like hands.

9

The red panda and the
ringtail are close relatives
of the raccoon.

Red panda

Two ringtails

Coati

The strangest relatives
of the raccoon are the
coati (ke-WA-ti) and the
kinkajou (KIN-ke-ju).

Kinkajou

14

Raccoons are good swimmers.

They can also climb trees.

Most raccoons live in the forests of North and South America.

They build houses called dens in hollow trees, tree stumps, or logs.

Their homes are usually near a pond or stream.

Many raccoons live close
to cities or towns.

They may look for food
in gardens or garbage cans.

Raccoons usually hunt
at night.

Raccoons like to eat mice, small birds, fish, crabs, frogs, corn, fruit, and insects.

A raccoon eating an apple

A raccoon catching a fish

During cold winter
months, raccoons only
leave their dens when
they are hungry.

There are no plants to
eat, but they can still
catch fish and small birds.

Young raccoons are born
in the spring.

A mother raccoon usually
gives birth to three or four
young at a time.

A newborn raccoon
weighs less than a fork.

Newborn raccoons

Young raccoons leave their den when they are about ten weeks old.

Then mother raccoons teach their young to hunt.

When the young are about a year old, they begin life on their own.

Words You Know

coati

den

kinkajou

mask

paw

ringtails

31

Index

About the Author

Allan Fowler is a freelance writer with a background in advertising.
Born in New York, he now lives in Chicago and enjoys traveling.

Photo Credits